Halloween Theme

By John Carpenter
Arranged by Michael Story

── INSTRUMENTATION ──

1   Full Score
8   Violin I
8   Violin II
5   Violin III (Viola 𝄞)
5   Viola
5   Cello
5   String Bass
1   Piano Accompaniment
2   Percussion
      (Hi-Hat Cymbals,
      Tambourine

NOTES TO THE CONDUCTOR

This timeless theme from the *Halloween* franchise is one of the creepiest tunes ever written. There should be a general sense of foreboding throughout. Although this arrangement has been written for string orchestra, easy piano and percussion parts are included, both of which are optional.

The long crescendos in measures 13–20 and 33–40 should be very gradual and restrained. Don't build up too much too soon or there will be nowhere to go. The biggest crescendos should occur in measures 20 and 40.

In measures 37–40, the upper divisi notes in the 1st violin are taken in 3rd position. It is totally fine, however, if these measures are played utilizing only the lower notes.

I hope you and your string orchestra enjoy *Halloween Theme*!

NOTE FROM THE EDITOR

In orchestral music, there are many editorial markings that are open for interpretation. In an effort to maintain consistency and clarity you may find some of these markings in this piece. In general, markings for fingerings, bowing patterns, and other items will only be marked with their initial appearance. For a more detailed explanation of our editorial markings, please download the free PDF at www.alfred.com/stringeditorial.

X	⁻	'	(♭), (♯), (♮)	⊓ ⊓ or V V
extended position	**shift**	**bow lift/reset**	**high or low fingerings**	**hooked bowings**

Please note: Our band and orchestra music is collated by an automatic high-speed system. The enclosed parts are now sorted by page count, rather than score order.

Halloween Theme

FULL SCORE
Duration - 2:00

By John Carpenter
Arranged by Michael Story

49917S

*Purchase a full-length
performance recording!*
alfred.com/downloads